Specific Measurable Results

90 Days to Success

Table of Contents

Book Description

Are you a manager who feels that your team has hit a performance plateau?

Are you a new business yearning for amazing growth?

Do you want to inspire your team out of their comfort zone to aspire higher and outperform themselves?

Are you simply tired of the usual goal-setting methods which do not seem to work for your business?

The objectives and Key Results (OKRs) framework is your answer! It worked for Intel, propelled Google from a startup to a global business and tech juggernaut, and has propelled many other businesses to great success.

OKRs are the answer for individuals, teams, managers, and businesses who want to outperform themselves to achieve results they never thought possible. Objectives and key results are a revolutionary goal-setting framework that identifies, defines, guides, and ensures that goals set are clear, well understood, and aligned to overall business strategy for positive outcomes.

"Specific Measurable Results- 90 Days to Success" covers the basic concepts of OKRs and how to implement them for different businesses.

You will learn:

- What objectives and key results (OKRs)are
- Concepts of objectives and key results

- Benefits of OKRs
- How to implement OKRs
- Why you should set amazing goals to get amazing results
- Common OKRs mistakes
- OKRs for small businesses
- OKRs examples for startups, Steps to successful networking
- OKRs tools and software
- OKRs and Agile vs. Waterfall Approaches
- OKRs case studies

This book covers the essential OKRs information you require to take your performance to the next level. You will be empowered with the goal-setting cultural and mental shift of OKRs to move you from regular goals to ambitious goals and from putting emphasis on input (work) to prioritizing outcomes (results).

I will also share my personal OKRs story and a success story of a client I work with.

Don't lose another minute! Come with me on this OKRs journey, and I'll guide you on your journey of setting ambitious goals and achieving outstanding results.

About the Author

Suresh was born in a refugee camp in Ulhas Nagar, Maharashtra, India. He started his career with a job that paid him only Rs. 300 (Approximately 4 USD per month). With pure dedication and hard work, he ventured into his own business of Apparels Export at the age of 21. This not only earned him crowning achievements, but he was also able to mushroom his making in multifold by 300 times oversubscribed IPO in 1995, and his company got listed at Bombay Stock Exchange. Apart from being a Presidential Award receiver, he is a Passionate Serial Entrepreneur and Investor. He has helped in laying the blueprint of many businesses and transform them into money magnets.

He is 63 years old, but his ambitiousness and 'keep moving forward' factor could make one feel as young and passionate as a 20-year-old. He has 43 years of experience (Tajurba) alloyed to his name. And during these 43 years, he had added many jewels to his throne of expertise.

Currently, he is on a mission to build the world's largest business network Tajurba Business Network. His vision is to create ten million SMEs as multi-dollar millionaires. His ideology backs this vision and mission that one should be a job creator instead of a job seeker.

Suresh has had quite an epic journey so far, with failures and fewer successes but big ones. Despite a volley of back-breaking shortcomings, he still carries a prideful smile on his face because he firmly believes that failures are the stepping stones that lead to success. So, let's begin with his biggest failure.

Failure

In the list of his failures, this was a big one. He founded online DVD rental MovieMart in the year 2006. He burnt the midnight oil for this project to succeed, but it kissed the rubble, and he lost a lot of his toiled money.

Successes

His first Start-up was at the age of 21. His company came out with one of the most successful IPOs in 1995, which was oversubscribed by more than 300 times. This accomplishment won Suresh the Presidential Award. He did not have capital, education, a mentor, internet, telephone, and most importantly, EXCUSES. Yet, he became a multi-millionaire at the age of 35. He believes either you have **Reasons or Results**

Today, Suresh is one of the **Best Business Coach, OKR Coach**, Certified **Gallup Strengths Coach**, Certified **Sales Trainer, Motivational Speaker**, and **TEDx speaker.**

He has trained over 5000 Business Owners from all over the world and helped them grow their sales and profits many folds. His tailored one-to-one Business Coaching sessions help the Business Owners who want to exponentially grow their sales & profits exponentially in just 3-5 years and become Unicorns.

Suresh can be contacted at:

suresh@sureshmansharamani.com

www.sureshmansharamani.com

What Led Me To Orchestrate This Book?

The reason behind orchestrating this book is that I see many people struggle to achieve their goals. Beginning of the year, the top management teams sit in the board room and decide the yearly goals and communicate to the department heads. Department heads, and the employees at the lowest levels have no meaning to company goals. There is no alignment.

After few weeks, they all forget about the goals, and at the end of the year, the blame game starts in the board room, and few key employees are blamed and sacked. The same story keeps repeating year after year without much progress.

On the other hand, companies like Google, Amazon, Walmart, etc., keep on growing leaps and bounds. There is one secret behind all of these companies' success, and that is the implementation of **Objectives and Key Results (OKR).**

On the other hand, the situation with small and medium businesses is worst. Some of them don't even set goals; they forget about setting yearly goals. They are only firefighting. Some of them in the search for answers end up with various business consultants and coaches, most of whom don't have any business experience.

Nothing happens and they feel frustrated with their lives and business. In the end, the only things they get from some of these coaches are Gyan but no execution; they offer bookish knowledge but no hand-holding, execution, or results for their clients.

I personally went through the same situation in my businesses, and when I became a business coach myself, I could feel this frustration amongst my clients. Even though they could grow exponentially under my guidance, that big spark was missing. I started studying how companies like Google and Amazon keep on growing exponentially year after year without getting impacted by any recession or adverse conditions. How startups like UBER, Airbnb become Unicorns within few years.

I found the secret. It was an eye-opener to know about OKRs. How simple and practical OKRs systems are. I started going deeper and deeper into it and learned everything about OKRs.

Another surprising thing I noticed was that SMEs (Small & Medium Enterprises) and individuals were not even aware of OKRs. My mind kept asking why it can't be applied to individuals and SMEs.

Please read the success stories at the end of this book. You will be better able to resonate with these stories after you have gone through the entire book.

Post your reviews on Amazon and show your love. Thank you and all the best for your amazing future.

Introduction

An objective and key results is a goal-setting tool developed by Andrew Grove, Intel co-founder in 1968 from Peter Drucker's Management by Objectives concept and has been used since the 1970s when it was first implemented at Intel. The experience at Intel of the **OKRs framework** was very positive because it opened employees' and management's eyes to how individual actions can have a great impact on organization goals and could be measured.

John Doerr, who learned it while working at Intel, introduced it to Google while advising the founders early in the life of the company. It is at Google where the OKRs framework was firmed up and gained prominence and is still used to date. Other companies like Airbnb, Dropbox, LinkedIn, Spotify, Twitter, and Uber have applied it to great success.

It is generally agreed that effective goal setting is the sure way to achieve desired goals, especially for businesses; however, traditional goal-setting techniques do not seem to be working for most people. One of the main challenges of the traditional goal setting techniques such as SMART is that they are not effective at managing many teams to work toward a common goal because they do not focus on "what matters."

Businesses can employ very good strategies to get them ahead, including injecting sufficient capital and attracting the best human resource; however, without the right culture of accountability and excellence, they stagnate or fail. OKRs framework is the right methodology to bring you a culture shift of accountability and better performance.

It is on the basis of these and other deficiencies that objectives and key results methodology were developed at Intel to cover these shortfalls and to optimize individual and team performance, and align different goals for the achievement of the company vision. With OKRs, you will no longer settle for normal goals, and you will easily get out of your comfort zone to consistently pursue amazing goals.

In the course of this book, we shall take a look at the basics of OKRs and how to implement the framework effectively for efficiency in performance to achieve amazing results. Each topic will equip you further to understand and use OKRs to your advantage. Included are OKRs examples for different businesses and some leading OKRs software and tools you can use.

So, let's get started.

SECTION 1

OBJECTIVES AND KEY RESULTS FRAMEWORK EXPLAINED

Chapter 1. What are Objectives and Key Results (OKRs)?

If you have followed the story of the growth and success of Google, you have probably heard of their performance management silver bullet- objectives and key results.

OKRs, objectives, and key results are a great way for organizations and individuals to set and achieve the most daring goals. Unlike other goal-setting processes, the OKRs framework is such that it compels organizations, teams, and individuals to come up with aggressive and highly ambitious goals.

Objectives and key results (OKRs) are a structured goal setting and management framework used for the implementation and execution of strategy and have gained popularity for their effectiveness in team collaboration and enhanced productivity. Objectives and key results (OKRs) are great for teams since it defines and sets outcomes with measurable results and known to everyone within the organization.

It is the quantifiable outcomes, which are key results and are used to measure how successful teams are in achieving their objectives. OKRs framework focuses on the impact of the respective functions for the realization of the overall organization objective, making it effective for vertical alignment of strategy. OKRs emphasize the value of every function contributing to the overall goal rather than emphasizing individual tasks.

It is an effective collaboration tool for teams to engage each other for the implementation of projects- it not sets goals but also comes up with desired measurable results, aligns the goals of different teams, and tracks progress. Objectives and key results (OKRs) work well for teams since it aligns and publicizes set goals throughout the organization- individual goals are aligned with team goals, and team goals are aligned with organization objectives.

The same basic principles of OKRs can be adopted and customized by individuals for the management of personal goals or individual functions within a team.

The advantages OKRs bring over traditional goal-setting methods are in its implementation and execution framework, which emphasizes results that matter, ensures better strategic alignment throughout the process, and is more transparent. This is made possible by marshaling teams and individuals within, and their respective roles in achieving common objectives agreed for achieving agreed key results.

Objectives and key results work by deciding on an objective, identifying key results needed to realize the objective, and putting into action initiatives to achieve the key results. It is an effective framework that emphasizes the achievement of identified outcomes (key results) rather than output (results) by bridging strategy and execution.

Characteristics of OKRs

Five core OKRs characteristics are critical for maximum impact and must be covered by everyone setting up the framework.

1. Ambitious

OKRs must be ambitious because the intent is to get you out of your comfort zone and push you to achieve bigger results than you are used to. OKRs have also been described as aggressive and action-oriented for this very reason.

As much as the goals you set must be ambitious, they must also be realistic. Set goals that are difficult to attain but can be achieved.

Define ambitious goals by answering the following questions:

- Have you written down the goals?

- Are the goals SMART?

- What is the timeline for the goals?

- Are they aggressive enough to get you out of your comfort zone?

- Are the goals daring?

- Are the goals divided into short-term and long-term?

- Are the goals geared to solve problems that most matter?

The goals should be precise for clarity and ease of understanding for those who will be implementing them. Ambitious goals boost creativity and performance and push us to achieve targets we did not think possible.

2. Measurable

OKRs must be measurable; otherwise, you would not be able to figure out how well you are performing. Key results set should be quantifiable but should also be flexible to be customized or quickly modified.

3. Simple and public

OKRs should be written in simple language and made available to everyone in an organization for easy understanding and execution. All organization, team, and individual goals should be shared so that everyone is on the same page and is aware of what the rest are working on. This openness promotes collaboration and alignment.

4. Aligned

Alignment means a concerted and focused effort by everyone in an organization to achieve common objectives. It allows individuals and teams to coordinate with others and link their objectives for the achievement of the ultimate goals. Individuals and teams, through alignment, share in the collective mission and contribute to its achievement. It also gives everyone involved a sense of ownership which makes them more engaged and innovative.

5. Long-term and Short-term

OKRs must be divided into clear long and short-term goals- the ultimate objectives being long-term and the cascaded objectives short term. Short-term goals are quarterly, while long-term goals are annual or longer.

Concepts of Objectives and Key Results

OBJECTIVE(S)

Question: "Where do you want to go?"

"What is your objective?"

- Sets a clear destination and direction to get there.

KEY RESULTS

Question: "How do you know if you have reached your destination?"

"How do you know that you have achieved the objective?"

- Shows and measures progress along the road to your set destination.

- Marks distance covered (milestones) and the remainder of the journey.

INITIATIVES

Question: "What do you need to do to get to your destination?"

"What do you need to do to achieve the objective?

The steps are taken to get to a set destination.

Objectives

An objective is a defined milestone set to be achieved and is usually action-oriented. Objectives are like a map. They direct an organization or individual to the future and should be practical and easy to understand for everyone involved.

The Main Characteristics of Objectives

1. Aligned

Objectives must connect to and support an organization's ultimate goal by linking individual and team performance to the main goals.

2. Aggressive and High impact

Aggressiveness is an important trait of objectives- they should be ambitious goals with a high impact and positive effect on the ultimate goal when attained. Aggressive objectives are not easy to achieve and serve to get you out of your comfort zone to make you perform better.

3. Time-bound

Objectives must be bound by time- they must have a clearly defined start and end. Making them time-bound ensures dedicated focus on them and allows review at the end of a set period. Time restriction allows for a change of tactic if the current is not working as deemed.

4. Clear and easy to understand

Objectives should be clear and easy to understand so that they are easily executed.

Key results are measurable benchmarks or outcomes necessary to achieve objectives- they define success or failure as defined by set objectives. They are measurable and quantifiable metrics linked to an objective for monitoring and tracking the journey to achieving set objectives.

Key results are like signposts on the road guiding you to your destination, which are set objectives. They have a specific set target to achieve and a defined timeline to start and end so that progress is easily measurable.

Key results must be realistic to attain but must also be aggressive to be effective- they should be specific, time-bound, measurable, and verifiable. Key results should be clear to avoid ambiguity.

The Main Characteristics of Key Results

1. High impact

Just like objectives, key results must be highly impactful to a set objective and the ultimate goal. They must be ambitious and challenging to create a noticeable impact on performance.

2. Target specific

Key results should focus on a specific target with a clear scope.

3. Time-specific

Key results must be time-specific and be able to measure progress for a specific period.

4. Ability to measure progress against objective

They should track progress and show measure how close you are to an objective.

Initiatives

Initiatives are the propellers used to get key results in motion towards an objective. They are the tasks and projects implemented for the realization of set key results. Initiatives are a very important part of the OKRs, which require a well-organized execution and monitoring process to succeed.

Alignment

Alignment refers to the process of linking respective OKRs within an organization. Think of it as a connection of company OKRs, team OKRs, and individual OKRs, which differs from the traditional method of cascading goals downwards from managers. Everyone involved works on individual key results rather than supporting others'- team and individual OKRs are linked to realize a set objective.

Cross-functional collaboration

OKRs success is founded on the effective and efficient collaboration of teams and individuals as compared to the traditional goal-setting processes where each team had and worked on its own goals. With the OKRs framework, all objectives are public to everyone within an organization, which enhances the collaboration of functions, thus negating duplication of efforts.

Grading

Grading simply means a metric of measuring key results. OKRs have a set deadline for review and attainment, which are generally measured on a scale of 1 to 10 to determine the progress of key results against objectives. The grading process should objectively evaluate OKRs and inform the next targets to be set.

Progress roll up

Progress roll-up in the OKRs process refers to the automatic roll-up of progress upwards, from the bottom level to the top. However, progress roll-up does not apply in all cases.

Types of OKRs

Objective and key results (OKRs) can generally be classified as industry OKRs and personal goal OKRs.

Kinds of OKRs?

Objective and key results are classified as either committed or aspirational.

1. **Committed or Qualitative OKRs** are evaluated at the end of a set time and are expected to be achieved.

2. **Aspirational OKRs** are also referred to as stretch goals and are usually long-term which outlive one OKRs cycle.

How OKRs Work at a Glance

The following is a summary of how the OKRs process works, by steps, to effectively create achievable objectives, achieve targeted results, and learn from results.

1) The organization's top management sets 3-5 ultimate annual objectives and breaks them down into quarters.

2) The objectives are cascaded downwards, and each team sets its own 3-5 objectives that are aligned with the top management's ultimate objectives.

3) Team members and managers engage in identifying 3-5 objectives and key results which should align with team and company objectives.

4) Managers and team members mutually agree on set OKRs and ensure that they are stretch goals that are not easily achievable and will give amazing results.

5) Ensure that OKRs are transparent and available to all in the organization so that everyone is aware of the bigger picture, is individually accountable, and can also hold each other accountable.

At the tail end, all participants will evaluate their key results and score them at the end of the OKRs cycle or quarter to monitor progress against set targets.

Benefits of OKRs

- **Business impact:** OKRs lead to greater effectiveness, better performance, and increased sales which makes it a better model for return on investment (ROI). One of the key benefits of the OKRs process is the resultant accelerated results and better performance.

- **Cultural shift:** The most important OKRs impact for business is the cultural shift from focusing on output to set outcomes. It increases performance and team engagement because it can be focused and aligned within the organization.

- **Employees' engagement:** OKRs have proven effective in engaging a workforce for a common purpose by simplifying the objective for everyone in the organization to understand and commit to.

- **Clarity and focus in execution:** Focusing on what matters is the foundation of OKRs- it emphasizes focusing and prioritizing objectives and initiatives which will have the biggest impact on business. There is clarity of roles and purpose in OKRs because everyone's goals are clearly defined.

- **Strategic alignment:** Aligning strategy to execution is another benefit of OKRs; managers and teams can use the tool to ensure that everyone is pulling in one direction. OKRs inform and syncs everyone's goals from the top management to the lower cadres, thus aligning everyone's work to the pursuit of objectives. Alignment connects all those involved to the company mission and positively impacts performance and results.

- **Continuous learning:** OKRs are a great opportunity for continuous learning, which leads to individual and team improvement. Regular OKRs check-ins afford an organization an opportunity for faster learning and improvement, which ultimately drives performance upwards.

- **Accountability:** OKRs is, in essence, a framework big on accountability at every level because of the regular innate monitoring and measuring components, which also track key results and key performance indicators, thus leading to improved accountability and execution.

- **Flexibility:** Flexibility is another great benefit. Unlike other strategic planning concepts, OKRs define shorter goal cycles, which allow teams to quickly adjust and adapt to change as they may arise, thus reducing risks and waste. OKRs objectives are usually set for a year, and tactical OKRs are quarterly, which gives room for flexibility.

Potential Challenges in Setting OKRs

Some challenges may be faced when going through the OKRs implementation journey, particularly if the goal-setting framework is being rolled out for the first time. Some of the common challenges you may be faced with in setting OKRs are discussed below.

Bottom-Up or Top-down OKRs?

OKRs are meant to be a mixture of bottom-up and top-down. In the initial stages of use, top-down OKRs are more common, but with time bottom-up OKRs increase as teams start contributing more confidently.

To avoid the lull at the beginning, high-level top-down OKRs should be set, then challenged, and objectives added that are yet to be covered by the top-down OKRs.

How to Measure Key Results

It is assumed by now that, as a reader, you know that key results should be measurable. However, when key results are set as increase sales by 15% or increase conversion by 12%, one may question if the indicated percentage is being measured against the previous month's sales or even the average monthly sales.

Precision is therefore important when setting the key results. For example, the above problems can be solved by indicating the key result as increase sales by 15% this quarter as compared to a similar quarter last year.

When to Measure the Key Results

When dealing with OKRs, progress is constantly noted to determine if any is being made towards achieving your goals and to make a prediction on what will have been achieved by the end of the quarter. For example, when implementing a goal that should be met by the end of the quarter, should the average performance of the quarter be used as the indicator of progress, or only the progress made after the feature is released will be relevant?

Precision is still the answer in this case. The key result should indicate exactly what is being measured, what the progress noted is being compared, and from what metrics the progress will be measured, e.g., after the release of the feature.

OKRs Cycle

A quarterly OKR mindset is great when it comes to focusing on important goals, especially from a product strategy and planning perspective. This may pose a problem when dealing with small objectives that need to be solved sooner or larger ones that will create a larger impact after the quarter has passed.

Short and high-priority objectives can be given a specified key result with its time frame. With the larger ones, you can include a smaller milestone with a lower impact.

Problem Solving or solution-specific

Whenever OKRs are set, individuals and teams expect to see the outcomes set reflecting in the OKRs cycle of the current period. A vague OKR will be unable to promote team accountability towards business results. Therefore, OKRs set should move from 'implement this' to 'generate this long-term business outcome.'

Identifying Key Results Involving Many Departments and Teams

When an organization is large, various teams or departments are working on objectives that may affect similar results. For example, product improvement by a team can affect marketing and sales teams.

The reverse can also be true in that when sales are high, and demand may increase, thus applying pressure on the market improvement teams.

To minimize the problems that result from this:

- Give the contributing teams the same goal

- Break down the goals into smaller pieces that the contributing teams can feel entirely in charge of.

The first approach is preferred because it increases collaboration between teams.

Cross-Team and Individual OKRs

When it comes to teams, e.g., product teams where there is a further breakdown of teams that are working on delivering results, it is not sensible to break down the outcomes into smaller individual tasks. OKRs are valuable because they offer visibility for teams on how they are contributing towards the achievement of company goals.

Company goals may not have a particular person responsible for them as compared to team OKRs, but the visibility they offer remains impactful. There can be a further breakdown into personal OKRs where progress measured is against an individual's contribution.

Cross-Unit OKRs

OKRs promote synergy within an organization. In practice, however, it should be noted that some areas will be responsible for driving some OKR requests to others. For example, a particular company that has a growth key result will need marketing to grow the business, and marketing will need product development to create a new landing.

This approach will go past bottom-up and top-down to the side-to-side approach. In such a scenario, conversation improves between teams as they may come together to prioritize and help each other achieve for the good of the company.

Short Goals vs. Broad Goals

Broad goals such as increase sales by Y% lacks focus and, in most cases, will only lead to marginal improvements. Having shorter manageable goals will ensure that teams work together doing small parts and having an incremental impact. When a specific area is identified for underperforming, teams will put more effort into ensuring there is measurable improvement.

Outcome vs. 'Processes & Practices'

OKRs tend to be focused on business outcomes. When teams need to work on a specific process such as experimentation, side by side OKRs have been added only to find that it is hard to compare and prioritize unrelated goals, and the process is lost when the objective is removed.

It is advisable to have only business-related OKRs at the team level. For improvement of processes and practice, make use of other types of evaluation and feedback.

OKRs, we should always remind ourselves is a learning process; there is always something new emerging to learn from so that we set better objectives and key results in the coming OKRs cycle for improved results. Additionally, being an open and collaborative effort, it is easy to deal with most of these challenges because of the collective efforts of all involved.

Chapter 2. OKRs versus KPIs

You may be wondering how objective and key results (OKRs) differ from key performance indicators (KPIs). At a glance, the two seem to be similar, but they are not.

Objective and key results (OKRs) and key performance indicators (KPIs) seem similar because they are both used as performance indicators; however, KPIs measure the performance of an initiative over a long time and are less goal-oriented, whereas OKRs are goal-oriented and specific with quantifiable outcomes.

So, key performance indicators are performance metrics used for evaluating the success of an organization or an initiative in an organization. Objectives and key results, on the other hand, outlines an objective and then define measurable "key results" to track progress and achievements of the objective.

The reality is that often, KPIs and OKRs overlap, but they are very different metrics. OKRs measure short-term business goals and overall objectives, while KPIs usually target individual daily performance. OKRs are clear and specific and track the progress of defined key results (short-term goals) for the realization of the overall objective. KPIs quantitatively measure and evaluate progress- usually individual progress.

KPIs measure performance in areas such as:

- Sales per employee
- Employee performance
- Customer lifetime value

- Monthly recurring revenue
- Customer retention
- Ticket resolution time
- Patient wait time

Examples of OKRs are:

Example 1:

Objective: Be a market leader in mobile money transfer.

Key Result #1: Record $20 million in revenue in 2021.
Key Result #2: Increase agents by 60 percent.
Key Result #3: Upgrade mobile money transfer platform by the end of March 2021

Example 2:

Objective: Increase revenue by 30 percent within a year.

Key Result #1: Acquire 500 new customers.
Key Result #2: Reduce advertising spend by 20 percent.
Key Result #3: Increase customer retention rate by 25 percent.
Key Result #4: Increase leads marketing and activation by 65 percent.

We can surmise that **KPIs measure outcomes while OKRs measure process.**

By differentiating lag and lead goals that are related to the two metrics, we will further understand the difference between KPIs and OKRs. Lag goals are used to define desired outcomes or objectives and thus relate to KPIs, while lead goals measure target values or key results used for the achievement of a lag goal, or objective relate to OKRs.

Leveraging KPIs and OKRs

It is important for every organization to regularly monitor and review performance because it is the only way to evaluate and improve productivity. Performance metrics should be a top priority for every organization- using both KPIs and OKRs leverages and optimizes the strengths of both worlds.

OKRs	KPIs
Objectives and Key Results	Key Performance Indicator
Aggressive and bold to realize an objective	A monitoring tool usually prompting action after evaluating results
Action-oriented goals (objectives) measuring (key results)	Number (metrics) measuring the health of a business
Are time and target specific, usually quarterly or yearly and change with the lapse of a set period	Are ongoing, and targets may change
Focuses on a future objective and is directional- moving from one point to the objective	Focuses on an outcome/result or can be a lead indicator tracking past results or future goals

The takeaway here is that OKRs and KPIs metrics are both important for performance management in organizations, but they are used for different purposes. They will reveal different aspects of a company's performance and success.

Combining the two will give a holistic view of organization performance. We should find ways of integrating their uses and leveraging on the two to measure and understand different aspects of a company's performance for better performance and productivity.

Where a KPI points to a need for improvement, it can be made a key result. For example, where a KPI indicates that dwindling sales figures, an OKR can be defined with key results of how to improve profits or boost marketing with the objective.

Use KPIs to help you identify inform what OKRs can solve- KPIs results point you to what needs improvement while OKRs set a long-term objective and short-term goals to get things on the right track.

Here is a plan of how you can use KPIs and OKRs together

1. Measure the most important KPIs to show past performance.

2. Based on KPIs results, pick out the most important indicators and set improvement targets as the OKRs objectives. Set goals (key results) to improve them.

3. Set specific OKRs timelines and update progress with the lapse of each key result.

4. At the end of a period, evaluate your OKR achievements against your grading metric. Analyze achievement for what worked and what did not.

5. Review KPIs at the end of very OKRs and note the changes. Set the next period's OKRs based on KPIs of the period ended.

No one method of combining the two metrics for measuring performance is guaranteed or is a standard. Every organization has a different set of unique challenges and objectives- learn the benefits of both and use them where they apply to you.

Effective optimal use of the two requires constant communication by those involved- the key for leveraging on the two successfully requires identifying challenges, sharing feedback, and discussing progress in real-time throughout an organization.

SECTION 2

THE PROCESSES OF SETTING UP OBJECTIVES AND KEY RESULTS FRAMEWORK

Chapter 3. Objectives and Key Results Process

"Deciding what matters" is the most important step of the objectives and key results process. Accordingly, every individual, team, and organization implementing OKRs should first ask the question, "What matters? What are the priorities for your strategy?

It is the identified priorities that become the main objectives and are realized through the action of appropriate shorter goals- key results. "What matters" then becomes an objective which then determines what key results will be defined to actualize it.

OKRs are valuable for performance management because they prioritize initiatives and define desired results from set goals. OKRs establish the objective or purpose and the desired outcomes an organization wants from key results.

The OKR formula as defined by John Doerr is "I will accomplish 'X' Objective as Measured by 'Y' Key Result." Accordingly, this formula should guide you in setting up your OKRs since the process relies on having measurable goals. It will help you to choose to decide the ultimate objectives and define how to progress, and key results are measured.

Preparing for Objectives and Key Results

Before you start implementing OKRs, there should be a preparation phase that involves the preliminary arrangements required to set the ball rolling for an effective, reliable, and effective OKRs process. The optimal cycle for OKRs is quarterly so that it gives everyone involved time to understand and get in a rhythm and to provide sufficient allowance for adequate reviews and course correction if needed.

Cultural shift

OKRs framework is a cultural shift in goal setting and performance management process to focus on the outcome rather than concentrating on output. The return on investment (ROI) for implementing OKRs is worth the time in the long run because it helps to get the most in terms of performance from individuals and teams, which in turn drives higher organization performance through ambitious objectives.

Conversely, OKRs strategic objectives are important in directing individual contribution because it crystallizes organization mission and vision into objectives that are easy to understand and execute. Properly defined and set up OKRs allow for seamless alignment throughout an organization for individuals and teams and also for interdependency across departments.

Alignment of objectives and goals is a powerful component that allows leaders to have substantial control in the way goals are executed and achieved but also allows individuals and teams to contribute to the realization of the ultimate goal. It is a collaborative endeavor that brings together top-down and bottom-up approaches to defining and achieving goals.

OKRs framework requires an organizational culture and mental shift and is a learning process. Everyone involved must be prepared for and requires a fundamental shift in how they approach and measure what they do- this process requires a focus on outcomes, not outputs.

Here is a step by step process to guide you as you prepare to implement OKRs:

Step 1: Define Purpose and Vision

OKRs are only effective in helping companies achieve their goals if team members know the direction a company should be going. A company director in the OKRs process is a higher purpose which will usually be a fusion of the mission and vision to motivate teams and allow individuals to align their efforts with company goals.

Step 2: Designate an OKRs Ambassador

One of the first things to do as you prepare to roll out OKRs is to identify someone within the organization to champion the process, and an Ambassador is also referred to as a directly responsible individual (DRI). One individual must be identified and designated to champion the OKRs process with the core mandate of managing the setup and implementation of the process by keenly monitoring and tracking progress to ensure that everyone stays on track.

The Ambassador is responsible for overseeing OKRs framework implementation and management throughout the process.

The ambassador's job is to ensure that individual and teams:

- Are well prepared and trained to implement understand the objective(s) of the OKRs framework being implemented.
- Are actively engaged throughout the process.
- Have assistance and guidance when needed.
- Follow set OKRs' best practices and plan.
- Define and set OKRs which sync with the ultimate goals.

The ambassador should engage everyone working on the OKRs, regularly check-in and follow up, steer and reign in teams to work within timelines, and report on the overall progress as well as the performance of different teams. This ambassador ensures continuous OKRs engagement and meetings for continuous process learning. The directly responsible individual does not need to be an expert but anyone in the mid-level cadre to learn and run with the role and ensure that everyone sticks to the best practices.

Once the ambassador is identified, the next step is to figure out "What matters," which are essentially the strategic priorities of an organization, which become the objective(s) or ultimate goal. To decide the priorities that matter, you will need to clearly understand the challenges you aim to solve and the benefits you expect.

Step 3: Conduct Strategic Session

It is important to have strategic sessions among the key people in the organization to set and align an effective OKRs rollout. These sessions should be conducted regularly- have an annual session and shorter ones every OKRs cycle.

Strategic sessions should:

- Review current OKRs progress.
- Analyze and evaluate important issues arising and make decisions on them.
- Define and align OKRs for the next cycle.

Step 4: Establish Acceptance and Trust

OKRs work well if those using them believe in what they can do and buy into it, which requires a culture shift within an organization.   Everyone should trust that it is a concerted effort towards common objectives and not about individual performance. Individuals should be free to give and accept feedback for more effective collaboration across teams and departments.

Main Components of the OKRs Framework

An optimal OKRs framework should have four distinct components to define goals and objectives, clarify the mission and purpose, and for seamless alignment of the process.

We can summarize the components of a good OKRs framework as follows:

- Focus and commitment to priorities
- Aligning and connecting
- Monitoring and tracking

- Stretching goals for amazing results

Focus and Commit to Priorities that Matter

In deciding "what matters," the management will be at the vanguard in defining organization strategy and vision, which will be the reference and driver of objectives and subsequent key results. Organization OKRs require top management to determine the overall vision and the direction they want for the organization, which must be clear through a vision and mission statement.

It is the responsibility of leaders to choose the priority objectives for the OKRs framework for a specific period by prioritizing and focusing on a few initiatives that are most likely to make a real positive difference.

After, the leadership should communicate the vision and mission vertically and horizontally throughout the organization. Let everyone in the organization know the "why and what" regarding organization direction and goal, respectively. This interaction brings clarity for everyone involved and helps them to understand how individual contributions and goals relate to the overall mission. The leaders should ensure that this interaction remains consistent and continuous.

In the implementation of OKRs, people need more than a set of milestones, and they need to understand how their individual and team goals relate to the mission. Leaders must be able to inspire true commitment, model the behavior for the success of the process, and lead by example.

The next step is to link the goals and objectives to measurable key results or mini-goals, which are the bridges to the objectives. While objectives are the overall or ultimate goals, key results are more specific, timely, and measurable and are supposed to be action-oriented and aggressive to push teams to achieve the objective. The better thought out an objective, the easier it will be to achieve and the fewer the key results required to get it done.

Priorities defined will require the establishment of clear timelines and timelines for the key results. Deadlines are the key and help to intensify commitment and focus- best cycles for key results quarterly even though it can vary depending on the objective. So that you are not lost in pursuing quantitative deliverables only, you should rope in qualitative ones to ensure that what is being delivered is substantively up to the task.

OKRs require an allowance for error so that you set flexible key results which can easily be adjusted or discarded depending on outcomes- keep in mind that OKRs are fluid and should allow for modification. Make the key results clear, specific, and measurable, and be selective in the way you set goals- the fewer the goals, the better because it optimizes focus and improves the chances of attaining the set objectives.

Of all the many activities or potential objectives, identify the most important to prioritize and concentrate on them.

Stretch Goals for Amazing Results

Organizations should continuously innovate to grow and prosper- sustained growth requires pushing beyond comfort zones and stretching the limits of what is possible. As pointed out earlier, OKRs should be aggressive and action-oriented, which is the connection to stretching goals and objectives for amazing results. When important and realistic objectives ("what matters") are identified and focused on, it is possible to achieve any desired goals- it is possible to aim for and achieve amazing results.

For stretched goals to succeed:

- They should not be top-down decisions- must into account realities and involve everyone.
- Leaders should convey the importance of the objective or outcome.
- They should not be rolled out too fast and too far-stretch modestly and realistically.
- They require the commitment of everyone
- Leaders must make everyone believe that it is attainable.

OKRs are the ideal tool for getting organizations out of their comfort zones and making stretched goals a reality. If stretched goals are chosen and set wisely, they enable more creativity and will unearth underutilized capacity, which can be a big boost in an entrepreneurial setting.

Achieving the amazing requires a transparent process and an organization that is well-aligned and connected for efficient collaboration. Stretching goals elevates focus and unleashes creativity which brings the best out of people.

Align & Connect OKRs to Objective for Teamwork

OKRs are a team-based goal-setting process where a shared objective and success are measured by the impact of the whole team and not an individual. Alignment and connection refer to the much-needed linkage of different players in the OKRs process to the objective. Individual and team activities and key results should be tied to the overall objective, and it is this linkage that is called alignment.

Alignment puts everyone on the same page with the objective and is key for OKRs success because it ensures focus in the right areas and makes it easy for progress monitoring. Without alignment, there can be a disconnect between execution and strategy.

Methods of OKRs Team Alignment

There are three main ways of approaching and achieving alignment for the successful implementation of OKRs.

1. Top-down OKRs Alignment

The top-down approach is the most used method for OKRs alignment. It refers to a system where senior managers set top-line objectives, which are subsequently passed downwards throughout an organization. Mangers down the ladder are responsible for ensuring that their teams focus and pursue the top-line objectives by coming up with relevant key results.

It is the go-to approach because it guarantees that the lower levels of the organization will stick to the chief objectives as set out at the top. However, because of the vertical approach and linkages, it does not allow for the much valuable agility and flexibility required for a robust OKRs framework because it locks out most of those in the organization from contributing to the identification and creation of the objective.

2. Bottom-up OKRS Alignment

This approach is the opposite of the top-down, where the lower levels players are encouraged to contribute to the overall objective, key results, and individual or team goals. This approach is healthy because it signals to the lower cadre that they are valued and gives meaning to their involvement in the process.

The bottom-up method is a motivating and all involving approach that benefits from innovative insights throughout an organization. An optimal OKR framework should aim to balance common purpose and creative latitude on one hand and alignment and autonomy on the other.

3. Cross-functional OKRs Alignment

The other method is cross-functional, which is good at tackling project slippage caused by a lack of peer-to-peer and team-to-team connections by establishing links between individuals and teams, thus connecting horizontally for better alignment.

This method enables better linkage for interdependent teams or departments within an organization and is critical today where organizations have grown complex, for enabling synergy of different teams while working independently towards the same objective.

Alignment and connectivity help to expose and eliminate redundancy of tasks, thus saving time and money. It inculcates and nurtures a highly collaborative atmosphere and clear goals and roles within an organization.

Monitor and Track Progress for Accountability

This a critical step in the implementation process- OKRs must be able to be monitored and tracked with ease so that it is clear whether set goals are meeting intended key results and objectives. A good monitoring and tracking option should identify problems so that they are quickly amended.

More organizations are adopting OKRs management software which is robustly designed for monitoring and tracking.

OKRs management tools should:

- Drive engagement
- Make individual and team goals visible
- Promote internal networking
- Save time and money
- Negate hurdles and frustration

Here are the monitoring and tracking phases:

Setup Phase

The first step is to adopt and set up a monitoring and tracking tool in the OKRs setup phase, and it must be adopted universally in an organization. Someone should be designated to shepherd this setup.

Mid Phase

After setup, the process enters the midlife phase, where the performance tracking tool monitors the input and output of everyone in the process and reports progress against key results and the objective. Check-ins or regular progress updates are important for the prevention of project slippage by quantifying individual, team, and organization progress against a target.

Depending on the progress reports generated, you will **continue** with the process if you are on track as projected and defined, modify and **update** to get back on track if there are concerns, **start** over with a new OKRs or **stop** if goals and objectives have been met or the goal has outlived its usefulness.

Wrap-up Phase

Then enters the wrap-up phase, where you will analyze the whole process and identify key lessons for use in the next OKRs cycle and requires three steps:

1. OKRs scoring: Which is an objective grading of what has been achieved to inform improvement in future OKRs cycles. OKR scoring is usually on a 0 to 10 and color defined:

    - Green   7 to 10   Delivered on target
    - Yellow   4 to 6   Short of delivering target
    - Red   0 to 3   Failed

If the OKRs are failing, a recovery plan should quickly be devised to get things on track.

2. Self-assessment: This step is a process where objective data is used for judging performance through subjective assessment.
3. Reflection: Here, you analyze and reflect on the whole process by interrogating results and key lessons.

The OKRs wrap-up is both a retrospective and progressive analysis step. It helps to decide whether an objective or goal should be carried forward to the next OKRs cycle or discarded entirely.

Importance of Continuous Regular Meetings

Regular OKRs meetings are important to ensure that the focus to achieve identified objectives remains at the forefront of the process and the priority of those problems. Meetings regarding ultimate objectives should be held monthly to review progress and alignment, modify objectives that are at risk of not being achieved, and thereafter declare action items and designate those responsible for those actions.

For cascaded OKRs, biweekly meetings are ideal not only to review and track progress but, more importantly, to identify and correct any errors or potential problems. Team OKRs meetings are the most critical because it is this level that is largely responsible for the failure or success of the process.

OKRs should be analyzed in-depth several times in a defined period, usually a quarter, at all levels so that progress is reported, hurdles identified and key results modified and refined. An integral part of the monitoring process is regular meetings to evaluate progress against objectives.

Monitoring and tracking help to identifies areas of improvement and for assessments to inform a better OKRs process in the cycle.

How to Implement Objectives and Key Results

There are no strict rules for the OKRs process, which affords organizations great latitude and flexibility in how they set up the framework to fit their unique business situations. There are no one-size-fits-all OKRs. Every business implements them in the context and culture of their respective businesses.

Here are the steps that will help you implement your OKRs:

1. Setting OKRs

What makes a good objectives and key results framework? As you begin the process of setting up the OKRs process, this is the question you should ask yourself so that you have an answer to guide you in its implementation.

OKRs should be flexible enough to be adjusted as priorities vary. Use OKRs to shape business objectives throughout the year and then customize individual roles and team projects from the set objectives. The essence of the OKRs framework is to enable everyone involved to approach every task with an awareness of how it links back to the higher objectives of an organization.

OKRs work well if they are well documented and are clear and specific for easy alignment- anything complicated that creates confusion will be a hindrance in the achievement of OKRs. Make them measurable and transparent and should not too easy or too difficult to attain.

Check-in on OKRs progress monthly and regularly evaluate to ensure that it is well on track as expected. At the end of every quarter, grade performance against specific objectives to arrest any problems and adjust them as necessary. Consider past performance when setting up OKRs so that the goals and objectives set are achievable and not demotivating.

Look into market trends to guide you in determining the key area to focus on- move with or ahead of the times to remain market relevant.

The following are how to go about setting objectives and key results:

Finding the Right OKR Cadence

The OKRs cycle or timeline is also referred to as cadence and is usually set annually for company objectives, while and individual and team OKRs are quarterly. Since individual and team OKRs are foundational and more detailed than company objectives, the shorter quarterly cycle is ideal for close and timely progress monitoring so that in case the key results goals are not progressing in sync with company objectives, the OKRs can immediately be redefined or modified to align to company objectives.

On the other hand, a longer time is ideal for company OKRs sing they are directional.

Setting the Ultimate Goal

The ultimate goal is simply a clear and simplified version of an organization's mission statement and vision consolidated to confusing one with the other. The mission and vision are ideally aiming for the same objective, which- the organization's ultimate goal to which all other smaller goals should be aligned and for which they should aim and contribute to realizing. The ultimate goal is a long-term goal, also referred to as a "Moonshot goal," was coined by US President J.F. Kennedy.

Setting Company OKRs

Company OKRs are created to steer an organization for a period of up to 3 years, with every cycle set at 12 months. Company OKRs are a few manageable goals, usually 3 or 4 targets that an organization decides to pursue and achieve within a year. The best approach to setting up company OKRs is to involve everyone's input when deciding what is to be achieved.

The objective of the exercise of setting company OKRs is to have everyone buy into the process and agree on what the organization should achieve within a year OKRs cycle. Have meetings and workshops with team managers and have them explain the strategy and solicit views from their team members on the things they think should be prioritized. It should be an all-encompassing process- collaborative and engaging.

Setting Team and Individual OKRs

Individual and team OKRs are set differently as compared to directional company OKRs and are meant to define tactics to be used by teams and individuals and the results they are expected to achieve to contribute to the realization of company OKRs and ultimate goals.

An all-inclusive OKRs process gives individuals and teams a sense of accomplishment, ownership, and direction and also has an opportunity to decline things that are not within the scope of the OKRs. Devolved OKRs processes lead to higher success and ensure that the strategy is implemented and the ultimate goal is realized.

Get Top-Management Buy-In

Just like the top management of an organization looks forward to the rest of the team buying into the OKRs they set for the company, Executive buy-in of OKRs down the hierarchy is important for strategy success. Top management should lead by example and are responsible for company strategic direction; without their interest, focus and priority, the OKRs would not work.

2. Tracking OKRs Progress

Monitoring and tracking is the next important step in the OKRs implementation process to ensure that everyone abides by the set key results and objectives. This step also requires regular meetings to discuss progress- this is important for both individual and team accountability to the ultimate goal. Consistent meetings to track progress also helps to align the process across departments for smooth interdepartmental functioning.

3. Reviewing OKRs

The current marketplace is quite dynamic, which is informed by rapid economic changes as well as fluid innovations which always influence consumer behavior. This is a major reason for the need for regular reviews of OKRs to ensure that organizational goals are not only achieving desired goals but that they are also in line with any changes, and if not, they are quickly modified to align with the realities outside an organization.

OKRs reviews analyze individual performance, assess team and company performance against the set objectives. Comparing your performance, goals, and objectives to industry peers is another lens through which you may opt to measure your OKRs progress. Regular in-depth OKRs reviews ensure that the process is effective and keeps OKRs on track and in sync with the company ultimate.

OKRs are designed to work for both individual and team goal-setting, in line with ultimate goals to help those in an organization prioritize work in a fast-paced environment, which is what OKRs are because it is aggressive and action-oriented.

One of the main de-motivators of employees in an organization is failure to reach set goals. For this reason, the importance of engaging everyone throughout the OKRs cycle cannot be understated. It is even worse when people fail, and they were not part of the discussion of what they were working on.

It is incumbent upon leaders at all levels to engage their team members in continuous and regular conversations to discuss the goals and objectives and to monitor their respective progress. OKRs help individuals and teams to see how their input is contributing to the ultimate goal- it increases clarity and better aligns the process. OKRs reviews also help with fine-tuning your framework in subsequent cycles for even better team performance and results.

Once the OKRs cycle is complete, you should evaluate the results and the process to identify what worked well and what did not so that you can modify the process and make changes accordingly. The post OKRs assessment process should involve everyone to find out if the objectives were ambitious enough. You should interrogate the key results and find out if any OKRs were ignored.

4. Scoring OKRs

Scoring comes at the tail end of the OKRs cycle when you need to assess and grade your overall performance for a period, usually a quarter. It is a time to reflect on your accomplishments and to figure out what you could do differently in the next OKRs cycle to perform better than you have. Generally, a low score signals poor performance and will force you to reassess your OKRs, while high scores reflect positive performance and reflect the delivery of goals and objectives.

The typical scoring scale is 0.0 to 1.0, which measures the performance of the targets set for the ending OKRs quarter. The lowest set target becomes the baseline; therefore, any result below the lowest target set is scored at 0 (zero) because it did not meet the minimum requirement.

Since OKRs are aspirational goals designed to push for amazing results, it is quite normal for scores to be in the average range of 60% and 80% - this score confirms that the team has performed beyond what they thought is possible.

OKRs scoring should be simplified as much as possible and should be flexible enough to rate objectively. For example, if you set to a target of 20% and attain 15%, score the performance at 0.75. Remember that scores are not equal to performance but are simply indicative of improved performance or vice versa and are a reflection of the effectiveness of objectives set.

If you have a consistently low-scoring objective, then you may consider changing it- maybe it is not the right objective for you. Conversely, if your objectives are consistently scoring top marks, you should evaluate them because they may be too easy, not aggressive enough.

Common OKRs Mistakes

The following are some common mistakes people make when setting up OKRs:

1. **Not Designating the OKRs Ambassador or Directly Responsible Individual (DRI)**

The OKRs ambassador, also known as a directly responsible individual (DRI), is an essential position because the individual is responsible for championing the process. The ambassador's role is to steer the process to completion and success and should be accountable for the process; therefore, without this person, there is a likelihood of confusion, incoherence, and a lack of discipline.

The solution to this omission is to ensure that one person is designated the role of DRI at the outset of the preparation stage before top management begins defining the ultimate objectives.

2. Defining Unachievable Objectives

This is a very common reason for failed OKRs. As much as it is encouraged that you aim for the amazing stretch goals, it also requires that you settle for realistic targets. The principle is to push yourself to perform very highly, not to set unreasonable and unachievable goals, and thus the reason for a need to discuss the process, think it through and engage everyone in the organization.

Ambition and aggressive goals are well and good but do not set impossible goals. What you should aim for is to challenge yourself to push further by settling for achievable objectives. Otherwise, the process will be a frustrating and impossible experience.

OKRs should be an all involving collaboration when setting out objectives at the top and key results as the objectives are cascaded downwards. Think of OKRs as a tool for encouraging progress, not necessarily achieving 100% success.

3. Mistaking OKRs for Tasks

Often, people tend to approach objectives and key results as tasks, which should not be the case. OKRs are supposed to be viewed as a measure of value-added, not tasks delivered or jobs completed. This is the reason why the OKRs process is keen on clarity of purpose and recommends engaging everyone for their views and understanding of the ultimate objectives for alignment.

Everyone needs to understand the difference between value-based and activity-based key results so that it is clear to them that OKRs are not tasks or activities, but outcomes or results- both objectives and key results are not tasks but outcomes. Doing something does not automatically equate to desired results or set goals- you can be busy but not achieving results.

As Google has aptly put it, "One thing OKRs are not is a checklist. They are not intended to be a master task like…" Use OKRs to define the impact the team wants to see and let the teams come up with the methods of achieving that impact."

Accordingly, you should be able to differentiate and understand that tasks are the actual things or activities you do, projects are initiatives made possible by your tasks and objectives, and key results (OKRs) is a desired ultimate goal which is realized through the implementation of several projects. Similarly, objectives are realized via several key results.

To ensure that you are on track, use a dedicated OKRs work management tool to track goals and activities required to complete key results and, finally, objectives.

4. Setting too Many Objectives and Key Results

This is usually a result of a lack of understanding of the OKRs process or unrestrained ambition when setting objective targets. You will remember that the main principle behind the success of OKRs is "what matters" – the top priorities, not all priorities. You have to start by deciding what the most important 3-5 objectives are out of the odd number of important objectives.

The fewer and more focused your objectives, the higher the chances of your OKRs success and the easier it will be for everyone to understand and accomplish their targets.

Do not pile everything proposed or desired into the OKRs basket, and there must be a limit to the ultimate objectives so that there is control and focus of the process as it cascades down. That way, the objectives, key results, and goals set at the team level are relevant and focused; otherwise, you set yourself up for failure.

Setting too many OKRs imposes a lot of work on the individuals and teams, which leads to frustrations, confusion, and loss of focus. In the endeavor to achieve much more, leaders have often made the mistake of taking on too many OKRs to push their teams to accomplish more, but in most cases, it is counterproductive. You are better off succeeding at achieving a few objectives rather than struggling to and failing to achieve many.

The recommended number of objectives per quarter is 2-3 when first introducing OKRs and 3-5 in a quarter generally. Assess the performance of the process to help you decide if you should increase, reduce or maintain the number of objectives you pursue in the next period.

5. Insufficient Key Results for Set Objectives

A common hindrance for OKRs success is setting insufficient key results to meet the targeted objectives both at the team level and the ultimate. Teams will craft a few necessary key results, which are often insufficient to meet the scope of the objective, usually in an attempt to avoid the difficult commitment required in the delivery of amazing key results.

Everyone must understand the mission of OKRs as defined by the ultimate objective and believe and commit to the process. Additionally, it is for this reason that continuous engagement and the designation of the OKRs ambassador are critical to the success of the process because of continuous learning, progress monitoring, and steering of the process.

Scoring key results is another critical component for measuring their adequacy and efficacy. However, it is still possible to score 1.0 on all key results but come up short, which calls for tweaking of key results so that their successful completion guarantees that the objective is achieved.

Key results, which are the measurable steps undertaken to achieve the desired outcome, the objective, must be relevant and sufficient to meet the intended goal. Key results require frequent assessment and review to ensure that they are on track and achieving desired results.

Without the right model and progress monitoring to ensure sufficient key results, it will be too late before it comes to light that they are inefficient and that the objective will not be met.

6. Top-Down Objectives

As we have learned earlier, a top-down approach for objectives does not augur well for OKRs success because it alienates those who are out of leadership contributing to the ultimate objectives. It is for the leadership to define the vision of an organization but, they must allow the rest to contribute to the objectives and continuously engage them in the process for clarity and understanding.

Cascading goals downwards is important, but there is a need to merge it with a bottom-up approach which allows the rest of the team to contribute and critic set objectives. An all-encompassing approach makes everyone own the process, while a strictly top-down approach curtails creativity and is demotivating. They should have a substantive say in the OKRs process which should be continuous- encourage them to action their OKRs to support company objectives. OKRs work best if they are collaborative for everyone to buy into the process and commit.

For creativity and high performance to thrive, the lower cadre should be allowed a level of autonomy. Since the lower cadre will be responsible for executing strategy, it is necessary to find out what they think should be prioritized for them to perform at optimum.

7. Lack of Clarity

Simple, clear, and measurable OKRs are the way to go. Avoid setting unclear goals which are unmeasurable and thus ineffective. Unclear goals, apart from being unmeasurable, are not easy to understand. There is a need for detailed and specific targeting to guide teams and to enable progress to be monitored and measured effectively.

Consider the following main attributes of good objectives and key results:

- What is the goal?
- By what percentage or any other metric should it be improved?
- The period for completion?

When the above aspects are clearly defined, it makes it easy for those handling them to know what they are targeting, what performance or improvement is expected, and the timeline for accomplishing it. Involve everyone and ensure that there is clarity of purpose and expectations- make goals specific and measurable.

8. Lack of Short-Interval Regular Progress Tracking

One of the attractions and reasons for the success of OKRs is the ability to track and measure progress frequently. It is recommended that there be assessments and reviews of the progress weekly to allow for any inefficiencies to be quickly identified and corrected or for the OKRs to be modified or discarded. Regular tracking and measuring make it easy for leaders to monitor progress effectively and promptly, which enhances performance discipline in teams.

The key is in the regularity of tracking and measuring progress. It also helps to identify the weak areas, which can then be improved upon. Track progress regularly and discuss it with the team without fail to encourage completion of set targets, for example, 10% of goals weekly for a quarter cycle. It also helps to keep everyone on track and aligned to the ultimate goals.

9. Not Differentiating between Aspirational and Operational Objectives

It is important to understand the difference between aspirational and operational (committed) objectives so that you can strike a balance between operational and aspirational objectives.

A misrepresentation or lack of understanding of the two types of objectives leads to confusion and failure. Additionally, planning for only one type of objective limits the ability of players to use their skills and strengths to realize goals.

Misrepresenting an operational objective as an aspirational objective can increase the chances of failure because there will be no clear understanding of the objectives to align their priorities. Conversely, an aspirational objective misrepresented as an operational objective makes teams defensive when they do not understand and cannot deliver the desired objective.

The solution to this is to involve everyone in setting OKRs, defining and clarifying OKRs, and double-checking and verifying to understand the differences and ensure a healthy blend of both types of OKRs.

10. Poor OKRs Resourcing

Inadequate resourcing or lack of resources is the easiest route to OKRs failure. OKRs processes must be well resourced in all aspects for them to run smoothly and successfully. Lack of adequate resourcing, is it financial or human, is a cause for frustration and can fuel resentment to the process, leading to poor performance or complete failure.

It is advisable to interrogate if you have enough resources to support the OKRs cycle to run its course. If not, you are better off mustering the necessary resources before rolling out the process. The alternative is to restructure the OKRs framework.

11. Fear of Aggressive Objectives and Key Results

This mistake comes in two limbs- giving the OKRs a business-as-usual or "who cares" approach or opting for non-aggressive aspirational OKRs.

Writing usual OKRs as opposed to opting for aggressive OKRs that lead to better performance is a weakness. Teams will mostly base their OKRs on what they believe they can achieve, which is growth and performance-limiting.

Successful OKRs require changes and improvement with every subsequent cycle- defining and setting more ambitious goals than the last to better performance and achieve more ambitious objectives. In any case, your OKRs should be upgraded to aim higher with subsequent OKRs cycles.

As far as non-aggressive aspirational OKRs, refrain from doing an introspection of yourself and opt for the better approach, which is to put yourself outside looking in to help you better formulate OKRs to define more daring goals for better performance and to allow you to achieve much more.

After navigating the process objectives and key results process in this chapter, let us delve into how the OKRs framework can be put into action for individuals and different kinds of businesses and organizations in the next section.

SECTION 3

OBJECTIVES AND KEY RESULTS IN ACTION

Chapter 4. OKRs for Individuals

Individual OKRs may be personal objectives or refer to goals set at the individual level in an organization and based on the idea that the work environment should move from one of control to one that is based on trust. In a company, the OKRs framework relies on everyone in a team aligning individual tasks to team objectives which are then synced with the company's ultimate goals.

Individual OKRs can be challenging to implement and align to company objectives because of the primary focus on the individual. OKRs for individuals are for the success of the overall OKRs and are set by individuals; however, importance is r given to team OKRs because they have different objectives and key results for a team, unlike individual OKRs that guide individual tasks.

Advantages of Objectives and Key Results for Individuals

1. Improves productivity

Individual OKRs improve productivity in a workforce since they help with ensuring accountability and transparency at all levels of the organization. Individual OKRs track the progress of each person against team objectives for validation enabling everyone to know what is important and how to do it faster.

2. Breaks down objectives

Individual OKRs break down ultimate OKRs into more manageable tasks for everyone. This encourages and motivates individuals by converting big objectives into simpler and manageable daily tasks.

3. Encourages independence of employees

Individual OKRs dictate what the employees are supposed to do, thus ensuring that they are more independent - not every task needs to be run past higher-ups because of common reference points for everyone in a company.

4. Assist with performance management

Set individual OKRs may be used by the HR team to track employee performance, an additional benefit as the OKRs were developed as a way to determine the work that brings in the biggest business impact.

5. Helps with progress tracking and problems identification

With individual OKRs, it is a lot easier to track individual and team progress to quickly identify and rectify problems. Individual OKRs indicate if progress is as it should be or if more needs to be done to meet the set targets and deadlines. It also designates tasks to ensure that all company objectives are worked on and are prioritized for importance. Since different people will be working on different objectives, it is easier with OKRs for individuals to determine and track actions to ensure set objectives are met.

6. Ensures a focus on priority objectives

Individual OKRs helps everyone to get back to tasks that are a priority by aligning individual tasks to bigger objectives, which also makes it easy to get back on track if one loses track. Tasks are defined and assigned according to priority, thus ensuring more time is dedicated to the most important objectives.

7. Encourages employee involvement

Individual OKRs ensure that everyone is incorporated and involved in the OKRs planning and implementation process. Individuals set initiatives that will be used to achieve set OKRs for individuals may be based on single tasks or a few key results, thus encouraging everyone to remain focused on achieving set objectives.

8. Promotes individual well-being

OKRs for individuals encourage employees to define their own goals, thus making them feel a part of the decision-making process and value. This increases individual performance and improves their mental health.

Disadvantages of Using OKRs for Individuals

1. Prioritizing individual performance over company OKRs

This may seem like a contradiction of the OKRs process, but it can be a problem. It is very easy for individuals to prioritize their OKRs over company objectives, especially where individual OKRs are used to determine performance. In such cases, individuals tend to concentrate solely on individual performance rather than their contribution to the collective performance, thus interfering with the achievement of company objectives.

2. Adds complexity

When individuals are introduced to OKRs for the first time, there is a lack of familiarity with it and may consider it an interference with the workflow as well as an additional time-consuming workload. OKRs require different levels of management, regular updating, and reviews which can add to the perceived complexity, especially in situations where company OKRs may prove inadequate. Managers also have the additional task of managing team OKRs as well as the individual OKRs that need to be reported on and supervised.

3. Derail the original purpose of the OKRs

In most situations where OKRS are not well implemented, individual OKRs tend to be perceived as and used for individual performance management rather than in support of ultimate objectives. Individual OKRs are generally more concerned with tasks to be done for a certain outcome rather than why the project is being done in the first place.

4. Limits employees to the 'how.'

Individual OKRs are mostly used to guide how certain objectives are to be met rather than leave the individual with the freedom to determine how to get to objectives and the goals on their own. The initiatives are meant to be used as a guide rather than the OKRs. They reduce employee autonomy and limit their determination of what does or doesn't work for the company.

5. Minimized employee appreciation

As much as individual OKRs contribute to the ultimate objectives, rewards are often provided to the actions that advance a company's goals rather than the individual responsible for the advancement.

Through research, it has been established that most employees look for opportunities for future growth, and the compensation being offered as the main factors when choosing to work for an organization. This means that if the rewards are not being offered to the employee for whatever reason, people are less likely to be enthusiastic about working for the particular company.

Key takeaways for individual OKRs are:

1. Let the individual decide

OKRs accountability lies in letting people take individual responsibility by making individual decisions. You cannot achieve success without delegating decisions.

2. Assign OKRs related to daily tasks

Individual OKRs should be related to a person's daily tasks- you want people to concentrate on what they are good at so that you get the best performance out of them. Introducing new roles and responsibilities means having people learn things anew, which will delay the process and can even make it fail.

3. Publicly decide OKRs

As much as an individual will make the decision, it is important that this is done with others in a team for awareness and clarity of what everyone has chosen to take on and to help align everyone's tasks to the main objective. Public individual OKRs decision-making also ensures that peers monitor and track each other's progress to help stay on track and within deadlines.

Most companies are coming to the realization that individual OKRs are unnecessary because they complicate workload in companies. They tend to end up as initiatives and guides of what needs to be done, leading to a preference for individual initiatives rather than OKRs for individuals.

Companies can opt to assign an objective per person to improve accountability rather than create OKRs for individuals.

In most organizations, however, OKRs have proved useful provided that OKRs are well implemented. In these cases, the majority of the employees view OKRs positively and quickly buy into the process.

Chapter 5. OKRs for Small Businesses

The OKRs framework is often associated with large companies and rare small and medium enterprises (SMEs); however, OKRs can be a great tool for small businesses for growth and survival and to marshal all within to move in the same direction for common objectives. Indeed, implementing OKRs in small businesses can improve performance and boost results.

Most large companies have made good use of OKRs, which has contributed to their improved performance and exponential growth. OKRs can even be more effective for small businesses if implemented correctly- OKRs ensure the effective assignment and alignment of tasks to objectives, track progress, and measure business outcomes.

Benefits of using OKRs in small businesses:

- OKRs **unify teams** in small businesses by providing common goals and objectives that unite a team and help them aspire to achieve businesses' common goals. Unifying for common goals means better efficiency and improved performance, which increases the chances of success.

- OKRs help with bringing **clarity of purpose** in a business by offering a clear direction and timelines to be followed by a workforce. OKRs further require that a business strategy is made public to all so that they are all aware of and are guided by the common mission. It offers direction and a road map at the individual, team, and whole business level for everyone.

- OKRs **improve communication** within a business since the framework opens up communication vertically and horizontally for everyone's views in the planning and execution of strategy. Everyone should contribute to setting team and ultimate guidelines and objectives.

- By streamlining various functions in a business, OKRs push individuals and teams towards achieving business objectives beyond their comfort levels, thus **increasing the growth rate**. With OKRs, there is more focus placed on growing a business. Thus, productivity will increase for all team members and therefore for the business.

- When OKRs are used in small businesses, chains of command and structures are quickly set up and slowly get complex with the subsequent growth of a business; however, the OKRs framework **stabilizes systems and optimizes strategy and planning**. The objectives and key results grow in line with the business mission, thus ensuring their stability and prevents collapse when business growth increases.

- **Review of business performance is much easier** when OKRs are implemented. In small businesses particularly, a review can be done as often as once every week.

- OKRs **improve transparency in a business**. From the top management to the lowest cadres, objectives are clear since they are made public. In turn, this openness of mission and strategy contributes to guiding and ensuring that a business is on the right track and what actions are being performed in the business at any given time are aligned to the set objectives.

- Using OKRs in small businesses helps entrepreneurs **balance the daily administration and management of a business**. OKRs are easy to implement within small businesses as they do not require a lot of resources for implementation. The outcome should end up greater than the output, e.g., employee hours. The budgetary allocation will be better spent on business activities that cost relatively less for a greater impact on the set OKRs.

- **Training employees** will be easier as it becomes easier to show new employees what matters most to a business and how to go about meeting the objectives.

Deploying OKRs in Small Businesses

1. Introduce the concept of OKRs

OKRs ought to be rolled out in an organized manner which will require you to design and make a plan and ensuring follow-through with everyone involved. The plan should include a timeline, the expected start date, a flow chart that will guide implementation, and strategies to be implemented to ensure the set objectives are met—train team members on how to implement the OKRs.

2. Create the objectives

Have a brainstorming session for OKRs to draft the objectives and key results that will dictate the coming OKRs cycle. Involve everyone from the outset for awareness and buy-in.

3. Checking in on your OKRs

OKRs requires frequent and regular review and monitoring – it shouldn't be rolled out and then forgotten only to be evaluated at the end of a set period. Best practice requires weekly or bi-weekly check-ins to evaluate progress and ensure that you are on the right path.

4. Grading the OKRs

There should be a clear guide on how to measure the objectives and key results to ensure that they are met. Remember, your targets should be exceptional and that the process is more important than the scores.

5. Conducting a team review of the OKRs

Everyone in an organization will need to be informed of the OKRs implementation plan. When informing team members of the implementation plan, emphasis ought to be given to the ways OKRs can benefit the business and employees.

6. Launch of the OKR strategy

Once everyone is roped in, and the plan is in place, the next step is the launch. It is not a once time affair but will take time to fully implement and requires close attention to ensure that it runs smoothly.

To ensure the success of the OKRs implementation:

- Have a designated person in charge of the OKRs implementation process who will facilitate assigning of tasks and breakdown of the OKRs.

- Ensure regular progress tracking and review

- Avoid associating OKRs with performance reviews as it may derail the process and limit employees. The goal of OKRs is to encourage new ambitious initiatives among team members; linking them to performance reviews will limit ambition since employees will only work to meet their performance goals.

- Keep the OKRs simple without too much information.

- Use measurable key results.

- Analyse the OKRs provided to ensure they are the ones best suited for your business at the particular moment.

- Ensure there is a list of resources that will be necessary for successful implementation, e.g., budget, lab time, and additional help from other contractors as may be required.

- Make a record for all objectives that are raised but are not being used at the time as they may prove useful in a later OKRs cycle.

- Ensure the deadlines set are realistic and can be met.

When setting up the OKRs framework, you should avoid:

- Setting objectives and key results that are vague and non-specific- when OKRs set are non-specific, it means that there are no clear numbers to measure progress.

- Describing the activities to be taken rather than the outcomes expected to meet objectives.

- Creating OKRs that are not ambitious enough. If the OKRs do not challenge participants to improve and achieve more, then they are not correctly defined.

- Intuitive grading- OKRs set ought to have indicators that can be measured precisely rather than the use of guesswork to measure whether the OKRs have been met.

- Meeting the highest ratings on all the objectives. Having high performance on all the objectives means that the OKRs set may be small and need to be more ambitious.

Small businesses need to meet several goals to grow, and in this regard, OKRs have proved to be a useful framework in helping small enterprises tap on human resource potential to effectively realize significant, consistent growth.

OKRs can easily be adjusted to conform to a business setup and to a business environment. OKRs is the goal-setting process for growing small businesses into big companies, as is evident with the success of companies such as Google and LinkedIn.

Chapter 6. Cross-Team OKRs

OKRs are good for creating a collaborative and highly productive environment for individuals and teams. By implementing the OKRs framework, collaboration and cross-function are encouraged, which in turn will improve accountability and goal alignment in the organization.

What are cross-team OKRs?

A cross-functional team is a group of people from different teams and organizational roles that come together for a common task or goal.

Cross-team OKRs, also known as shared OKRs, are advanced techniques found in the OKR methodology and help different teams in an organization align for a common purpose. Various teams will share an OKR but will have different initiatives that are all aimed at meeting the set objective.

Setting-up Cross-Functional Team

Step 1:

Discuss the OKRs with the team and ensure that the whole company is informed on the OKRs to be used.

Step 2:

Pick a tool that will help you better manage the OKRs. Spreadsheets can be one such tool. With a good tool, tracking and managing goals are made easier. OKRs tools outline previous mistakes to help teams avoid repeating them.

Step 3:

OKRs evaluation. OKRs generally include time restraints. Revisions should be made regularly, e.g., quarterly or biannually. The frequency will be dictated by company demands.

Step 4:

Breakdown of the objectives. Organization targets should be determined first. The targets are based on guidance from the executive. The management team can thereafter hold meetings with other employees to break down objectives that match set targets.

Step 5:

Individual contributions. OKRs are broken down into tasks that are assigned to every team member. The individual will be required to show how much progress has been made to fulfill the assigned task.

Step 6:

Making a governance team. Cross-functional research groups can be ineffective because of a lack of clear leadership, accountability and are unable to prioritize the cross-functional initiatives. This is because they lack a structural approach. Having a governance team will help the team improve on collaboration.

Step 7:

Communication and follow-up. Evaluate the objectives set against the outcomes reached. Analysing progress dictates what changes and modifications need to be made for the targets to be reached.

Benefits of Cross-Team OKRs

1. Reducing information silos

OKRs may end up being challenging to report on as they are dependent on other teams and departments in a company. With minor modifications to the OKR cycles, alignment can prove difficult, and teamwork becomes challenging. Cross-team OKRs let different teams work collectively to achieve a goal, thus avoiding last-minute scrambling to achieve goals.

2. Increase in collaboration

Cross-OKRs encourage skill matching in the organization intending to meet and achieve company OKRs. Sharing the OKRs helps to identify the objectives that are most important and prioritize them.

3. Work mapping

In a company, the OKRs set is not only for a single team or department but are strategic goals and initiatives that apply to the whole organization. With cross-team goals, the work that should be done for the achievement of objectives is clear, and progress can be tracked.

4. Reducing the number of OKRs needed

Over time the OKRs can be overwhelming as constant adjustments are being made whenever the targets are reached. Teams that are in isolation may be working on the same objective without realizing work is being duplicated. Cross-team OKRs help to streamline tasks to avoid duplication.

5. Helps with decision making

With a team having different skills working on a common objective, it is easier to meet targets and work on challenges as they arise. Strategic decisions are easily made as the objectives are being approached from different points of view.

Best Practices for Cross-Team OKRs

- When working with cross-team OKRs, it is advised that you prioritize objectives, get rid of silos, and advocate collaboration to help you achieve your goals.

- Deal with the outcomes before the skillsets that are needed. Address the most critical outcomes and then come up with actions that will support the intended outcome.

- Cross-team OKRs should undergo pilot testing before the methodology is implemented throughout the organization.

Here is an example of cross-team OKRs:

Objective: Increase revenues
Assigned to: CEO
Session: Annual OKRs 2019

Key results:

- This objective has the key results below that will be assigned to different teams.
- Achieve at least 15% month-over-month growth

Assigned to: Sales
Reactivate 45% of the existing customers
Assigned to: Customer success
Analyse gathered data
Assigned to: Jane, Data Analytics

OKRs for cross-functional teams encourage collaboration, focus, and transparency on priority objectives. The collaboration and scheduling of strategy discussions are easier when the information relating to the cross-team OKRs is centralized. Cross-team OKRs enable you to track the performance of different teams and measure progress made on different objectives centrally.

Chapter 7. Information Flow in Organizations with OKRs

In organizations using the OKRs framework, performance is key, and there is pressure placed on meeting the set targets within a set time frame. Employee performance is dependent on good information flow in the organization for clarity of purpose and to ensure that tasks and objectives are well-communicated and understood.

Analysis of team dynamics and performance requires listening to employee stories to get insights that metrics alone cannot convey. Getting employee feedback is also important when working towards a common goal.

Therefore, it is important to encourage and improve communication as it is the only way to ensure information flow, which is critical for improved performance of individuals, teams, and departments. It should, however, be noted that communication systems that work for one organization may not work for another.

Three communication habits are important when trying to successfully manage a business:

1. Creating priority objectives that are broken down into individual initiatives that support the goals of the organization.

2. Having adequate data and information that will help come up with insights and performance metrics for every objective being handled by the employee. There should also be measurable results that are easy to track and update.

3. Ensuring the organization is aligned for accountability and effective communication. This is done by implementing a feedback rhythm that enhances growth.

By encouraging a free flow of information in an organization, trust is easily established. Soliciting feedback from employees does not just ensure that information is gathered but also ensures that actionable valuable information is passed along.

Importance of Information Flow in the OKRs Framework

- **It allows for quick assessments-** With information flow, managers can quickly and easily discover alignments and course-correct as needed.

- **Encourages teamwork-** When information is shared within the organization, managers and team members can know when an employee is facing challenges and offer adequate support to reach the shared goals and objectives.

- **Recognition-** Employee victories are acknowledged and rewarded, thus boosting the workforce morale. Rewards motivate others in the organization to improve performance.

- **It helps reduce operations costs-** An informed workforce tends to be more productive, engaged, and less likely to switch jobs. This helps with the reduction in hiring costs.

- **Efficiency in performance of duties-** Organizations with clear communication lines also have good information flow. More time will be spent on OKRs performance rather than following up on misinformation problems or access problems where what is sought is information the employees should already have access to.

Information flow is easier when the business is starting or when it is still relatively small. The growth of the business will increase the complexity of organizational interactions, and communication will be more difficult. As businesses grow, poor communication can easily result in low productivity and destroyed workflow.

Information flow is generally improved with the implementation of OKRs, and when OKR software and tools are used, communication and monitoring of progress made towards different objectives are made much easier. OKRs bring a workforce together to achieve shared goals.

Despite the benefits accompanying the use of OKRs in organizations, employees may still be hesitant to make use of it. Awareness and training sessions should be carried out before the OKR system is introduced and fully implemented in the organization.

After implementation, company-level objectives should be set first and then communicated to the rest of the organization, along with discussions on why the objectives are important. After, team OKRs are set with the company OKRs as a guide.

Additional information will be needed when analyzing the given metrics to determine context and what actions should be taken based on the determined patterns and projections. When looking at the OKR metrics, it is important to look at employee behavior that leads to noted results.

For OKRs success, communication and information flow should be improved throughout an organization. The recurring themes for OKRs success are creating objectives frequently, e.g., every quarter, implementing metrics that will be used to measure progress, communicating during the journey to meeting the set objectives, the discussing the successes and failures what changes should be made within the set period. These actions make the organization's goals easier to achieve.

Managers should identify the most effective and strategic communication channels. The most practical internal channels and techniques will help to ensure that the workforce is motivated and is performing tasks that are in line with set objectives.

Once full transparency is achieved in an organization, and there is focus and prioritization, financial progress is easy to track. OKRs improvements are not only limited to communication and information flow but will extend to other aspects of the business. OKRs accommodate and quickly adapt to changes that come with ambitious business growth.

Chapter 8. OKRs and Agile vs. Waterfall Goals

Organizations often find it challenging to use OKR and Agile together, even though the two are similar in approach and make for a potent combination for business performance and growth.

Many companies that use the Agile framework do not implement OKRs because they find them redundant. This, however, is not the case because when the two methodologies are used together since they can result in highly driven teams, positive company transformation, and adaptability and innovation.

Agile is a framework that was initially created to deliver software as an alternative to waterfall development which was the preferred method for managing software projects. Agile focuses on managing the features rather than the expected outcomes while tracking the process in its entirety. In most companies, Agile is mostly used for deliverables rather, i.e., output rather than outcomes which are the business problems the output is meant to address.

The waterfall goals that Agile has sought to replace follow a static planning concept. This means that the company's executive will come up with company goals which are passed down to different levels to outline the fixed plan for the year.

This framework, however, retains the following assumptions:

- Detailed plans can be defined in advance
- For the most part, the plan will be right
- Market conditions will not change
- If there are any industry changes, they will be minimal

With this approach, goals are not based on value but rather on planning work adapting hard while increasing waste and risk.

Agile differs from waterfall in that a principle mission statement will dictate what company actions are taken rather than using controlled detailed plans that are put in place by the executive. With agile, constraints are vastly reduced as the strategy is data-driven and is focused on validating different hypotheses. Tactics in this approach include experiments with short feedback cycles.

For companies to change and focus on practical actions, tools can be implemented to facilitate the change from a waterfall to an agile approach. One tool that can be used for business agility is OKRs which is a popular goal framework already implemented in companies like Google and Spotify, among others.

Unlike the previous planning methods, OKRs are generally set then revised frequently (in most cases quarterly) to adapt and align with company goals. OKRs breakdown of company mission into team and department OKRs, whose progress is overseen by managers. This method increases engagement and collaboration between teams. The progress made on the objectives is tracked to ensure changes made where necessary.

Common assumptions hindering the implementation of Agile in Waterfall based approaches:

1. The assumption made by different companies that individuals and teams are not capable of deciding what to build.

2. Teams are not working towards a goal but are instead performing tasks because it's what they feel like or should be doing.

The Agile approach is based on outcomes, and so is the OKRs framework, and that's why they tend to be easily misused. It is important to keep in mind that goals have to reflect a focus on value, particularly what customers find valuable. Value-based OKRs tend to help bridge the gap with Agile as well as the bridge between company product and engineering.

When OKRs are used together with Agile, they provide the experiments that teams use to learn and adapt. Teams will review the metrics derived from the OKRs, take a look at the hypotheses and work on improving them.

With this approach, a team is not limited to particular tasks but rather given room to decide how to go about getting the desired outcomes.

OKRs, therefore, compliment Agile by:

- **Creating a results-focused environment**. Agile focuses on managing deliverables rather than business results. With the use OKRs, the Agile approach can change from output focus to outcome focus.

- **Enabling self-organizing teams**. OKRs change the role of teams in an organization from delivering what the company executive wants but rather achieving the OKRs that are jointly set by stakeholders and the company teams.

- **Adopting value-based structures**. Agile as an approach does not account for results tracking. By using OKRs, agile teams can track progress regularly, prioritize the backlog based on what will quickly help achieve the OKRs.

- **Supporting Agile transformation** with the replacement of predictability with results. One of the shortcomings of Agile is the loss of perceived predictability. OKR helps with overcoming this by ensuring there is a commitment to deliver the predefined key results.

- **Incentivizes a breakdown of objectives into smaller objectives, tasks, and initiatives**. With the use of value-based OKRs, there is a commitment to reach the key results within the specified time limits. This will allow metrics that show the impact of different actions and what should be changed to meet the objectives.

Using OKR and Agile together is challenging, but both approaches can be leveraged to create a working environment that prioritizes delivering value rather than tasks. It is important to note that teams do not necessarily have to implement the waterfall plan that is created and established by stakeholders but instead find value in using the Agile approach.

SECTION 4

OBJECTIVES AND KEY RESULTS: EXAMPLES, SOFTWARES & TOOLS

Chapter 9. OKRs Examples for Start-Ups

Objective and key results frameworks are useful for any organization, particularly start-ups. OKRs are meant to encourage focus and alignment in an organization through broken down and targeted goal setting. It is a proven process and has been used with great success by start-ups to promote ambitious performance and increase growth.

Growing a startup is a difficult undertaking fraught with insufficient resources and uncertainty, competition from established players, inexperience, etc. that is why operational excellence is important. Start-ups require a good foundation to ensure the growth and performance of the organization are consistent and stable.

The OKRs framework lays a foundation for the business to grow while accounting for and embracing changes that come with growth and the increasing complexity of the organization.

OKRs help with tracking different outcomes for a start-up. Unlike a start-up without the OKRs framework, one using OKRs not only encourages its workforce to increase productivity but also provides direction while making them understand the ultimate goal.

Before setting up the OKRs framework, ensure that there is a general understanding by every one of the business, its purpose, and priorities. Additionally, have systems in place to track progress and measure performance. For OKRs to be successfully implemented in a start-up, various steps should be taken.

Stages of Adopting OKRs Framework for Start-ups

1. **Coming up with a vision and creating a vision document**

The start-up will need to have a clear outline of its end goal or expected outcome from performing certain actions. A mission statement should be outlined in a clear and precise manner. The vision document will need to include a focus area that indicates the objectives to be given priority.

2. Keeping up with the progress made and tracking outcomes and outputs

Metrics need to be put in place to determine if the set goals and objectives are met and at what rate. There are various easy-to-use tools such as Excel spreadsheets and other software that can be used to track the outcomes provided they are measurable. Tracking systems ensure that modifications can be made to accommodate new goals once goals are achieved or if there are industry changes.

Some of the best practices used when tracking OKRs are:

- Make tracking a team activity to ensure all employees are up to date on progress made and outcomes.

- Ensure that trends being noted are accessible to everyone.

- Automate the OKR process to encourage simplicity, standardize the process and reduce the tasks that will require the OKRs framework to perform.

- Having an actionable score.

3. Share progress

Progress made towards achieving the OKRs should be regularly updated and publicly shared. An appropriate system prompts employees to update individual progress made in the quest to achieve the organization's goals.

4. Making adjustments

Adjustments will be made to reflect progress. If progress is slow, adjustments will need to be made to ensure the goals are more attainable. The goals should also be ambitious enough to encourage productivity.

When using OKRs at the early stages of a start-up, the objectives must be focused on building an appealing product or service that will satisfy customers. Priority objectives in start-ups are those that will encourage customers to keep using your product or service and remain satisfied with their experience using the product.

Some of the actions that can form priority objectives will include making access to your product or service easier through simple sign-ups and activation. Objectives that are aimed at optimizing acquisition channels are generally set later on when the start-up is on a better footing.

Examples of OKRs being implemented in start-ups:

Example 1: A company looking to increase recurring revenue

Company objective: Increase recurring revenue

Key Result: To increase the number of new sales every week to XX

- You will therefore need to increase retention to X%

Product Management Objective: Launch the new products

Key results: Get X sign-ups
- You will need to increase free trials to increase the subscriber conversion rate.

Example 2: Customer satisfaction

Objective: Research and improve customer satisfaction

Key results: 8/10 through use of the tracking system.

The actions taken may include:

- Get 1000 survey responses to the annual satisfaction survey.
- Conduct 50 phone interviews with top customers.

Example 3: Marketing

Objective: Dissemination of content effectively

Key Result: Publish a (particular) blog post

Key result: Acquire an increased percentage of backlinks as compared to the previous months.

Key result: Gather an increased percentage of followers on different social media platforms.

Key result: get acceptance into a (specific) number of publications.

Using the OKR framework in start-ups brings incremental success, which in time results in long-term success and growth.

Success with OKRs is a result of the discipline and objectives-based outline that dictates what is to be done for the consistent growth of a company. The effort is directed towards the priority objectives to ensure that they are met within the set timelines.

Chapter 10. OKRs Examples for HR Company

As with any company, OKRs are a useful tool for both HR companies and teams, for setting goals in collaboration with other departments and teams. OKRs make it easier for the HR team to track the progress and performance of employees, ensure alignment of tasks and objectives, and generally ensure that tasks carried out in an organization bring it closer to achieving company OKRs.

Since OKRs ensure that a workforce work with purpose, it makes it easier for the HR department to perform their duties. Cross-communication between departments and teams, as well as outcomes and outputs, bring together valuable information for HR teams which is significantly improved by using OKRs. Synergy in a workforce eases HR workload.

HR tasks are, in most cases, qualitative and hard to measure, which makes OKRs quite useful in human resource work.

Example 1: Performance-related OKRs

Objective: Increase team performance

Key result:

- Increasing team performance by 55% percentage. (It could also be range, i.e., from X% to Y %)
- Increase participation in weekly check-ins by a 45% percentage

Example 2: Improve corporate culture by improving communication

Objective: Improving communication in the company
Key result:

- Improve the score by 65%
- Launching a two-way feedback process loop
- Acquiring 55 feedback entries

Example 3: Performance management

Objective: Improving the performance management process by the end of FY 2020-2021

Key results:

- Initiation of continuous feedback
- Increase positive feedback from surveys by 85%

Example 4: Employee engagement

Objective: Increase employee engagement 3rd Quarter Year 2016-2017

Key results:

- Reduction in absenteeism by 50%
- Productivity increase by 50%
- Increase in self-development initiatives by 45%

Example 5: Onboarding process

Objective: Improve the onboarding process

Key results:

- Conducting 25 interviews to find out the shortcomings of the onboarding process in place
- Increase in newcomer pass rate from 75-85%
- Increase onboarding satisfaction rate to 85%
- Creating a responsibility guide that encourages mentorship

Example 6: Improving working conditions in the company

Objective: Become the best place to work in the country

Key Results:

- Decreasing employee turnover from 18% to 8%
- Identifying problems in the company by conducting exit interviews with staff
- Address the personal development goals of staff
- Conduct manager and team training activities

Example 7: Improving manager relations in the company

Objectives: Making Managers effective and successful

Key Results:

- Increasing manager participation in manager training to 85%
- Implementing management training programs
- Conducting anonymous surveys on employees to determine how effective the managers are
- Implementing manager reviews, creating performance reports, and providing the performance reports to the company executive

Example 8: HR objectives for Compensation

Objectives: Improve the benefits program significantly while working within the budget

Key Results:

- Maintaining benefits budgets below $1000 for every team member per year

- Evaluating benefits programs of other local companies, select and design a contract with a vendor that best suits department needs
- Ensuring there is a 20% increase in employee participation in the benefits program

Example 9: OKRs for education and training

Objective: Implement personal development programs for all team members

Key Results:

- Achieve an 85% completion rate for the personal development programs
- Create a career outline for all 54 current positions and get approval from all team leads
- Create a program for all team members who are part of the personal development program
- Select a tool that will help track all PDP members progress and achieve a 90% satisfaction rate

Example 10: Significantly improve employee retention

Objectives: Improve employee retention rates

Key results:

- Conduct a survey to determine methods that can be used to improve transparency and alignment.
- Create a report outlining the comparisons between compensation being offered by the organization as compared to market rates for the same position.
- Improve average employee satisfaction to a rating of at the very least 8.5 on a rating scale of 1-10.

Example 11: Leave Management System

Objective: Create an effective leave management system

Key Results:

- Hire an assistant that will be tasked with working on employee administrative needs
- Evaluating different systems for leave tracking and choosing the system that will best serve the determined needs
- Implement the leave tracking system that has been settled on
- Achieve a 95% satisfaction rate with the new system

It is easy and tempting to associate OKRs with performance reviews in HR. However, this should not be the case since performance compensation based on OKRs leads to low targets that are easy to achieve, a decline in collaborations since individuals' need to achieve personal targets will supersede company objectives.

OKRs can be a consideration in performance reviews, but they should not be a significant part of the review.

Chapter 11. OKRs Examples for a Manufacturing Company with Multiple Departments

OKRs dictate alignment and productivity within an organization. OKRs pair objectives with measurable results that are limited by the time needed to achieve the objectives. Objectives will dictate the direction you want the company to head, while key results are quantifiable and show the rate at which the goals are being and should be met.

The following are brief examples of OKRs in major company departments:

1. Team OKRs

There are various teams in a company, and different teams can be in one department or across departments depending on team functions.

Example:

Objectives: Increase sales funnel by 55%

Key results:

- Increase the number of salespeople by 5%
- Reduction of lead posts by 25%
- Targeting 50 daily lead conversions

2. Marketing

Marketing in many organizations, particularly manufacturing companies, tends to take on a long-term approach. The marketing team is therefore encouraged to use OKRs to help with aligning goals within the department and cross aligning with other departments.

Example:

Objective: Creating a clear targeted content process to increase the marketing pipeline.

Key result:

- Conducting research using a focus group in the 2nd Quarter
- Decreasing the time taken between awareness and making purchase decisions by 20%
- Carrying out of a SWOT analysis of the two closest competitors

3. Sales

The sales department is tasked with meeting set revenue numbers to ensure growth and profit. Sales department OKRs define department goals to guide performance.

Example:

Objective: Increasing sales by 25% in the 4th Quarter

Key results:

- Conducting a survey to determine how to improve and personalize the sales approach
- Carry out check-ins weekly with potential buyers

4. IT department

The IT industry is constantly changing, and this requires constant change in the department to accommodate emerging innovation and technology. By implementing OKRs in the department, it will remain organized, and the department objectives will line up with industry developments and company objectives.

Example:

Objective: Securing digital platforms for use by employees working remotely

Key result:

- Generating e-reports that show security analysis
- Audit the systems monthly to ensure performance is up to par
- Making use of all the backup solutions

5. Executive

In a company, the Executive sets the direction that is taken by the entire workforce. Executive OKRs determine and guide the OKRs that are cascaded and implemented downwards in a company, as well as the corresponding objectives breakdowns used in teams and departments.

Example:

Objective: Attract the best talent in the Manufacturing industry

Key result:

- Increase internal company promotions by 40%
- Decrease employee turnover by 15%
- Conclude childcare program by the end of the 3rd Quarter

6. Human Resource

Human resource in the manufacturing industry is responsible for talent acquisition and recruitment

Example:

Objective: Improving the talent pool in the company

Key results:

- Increasing the minimum score for job application from 75% to 85%
- Increasing offer acceptance rate to 90%
- Reducing application submission date to response date by 45%

7. Finance and Accounting

Example:

Objectives: Improving accounting processes by building planning engines and improving business growth

Key results:

- Increasing quantifiable savings to 500,000
- Increasing capital efficiency ratio to 3.5
- Achieving ten-day close on the quarter

8. Engineering

The department may develop team-level OKRs that are a breakdown of the company OKRs. The objectives associated with this department tend to be prioritized when the company's main purpose is manufacturing.

Example:

Objective: create a high performing engineering team

Key results:

- Create performance metrics to be used in the department
- Encouraging every member of the department to participate in at least one industry competition per year
- Hiring nine new engineers by the 3rd quarter of the year

9. Project management

The project management department is where the least bit of data can decide the success rate of a project. OKRs ensure that projects stay on track and are not derailed.

Example:

Objective: implementing agile project management within the company

Key results:

- Deploying the agile method parameters by the end of the 1st Quarter
- Hire agile methodology coaches to train employees on its implementation and use within the company by the 2nd Quarter
- Ensuring that all the projects in the Engineering Department are wholly agile by the end of the 3rd Quarter

10. Customer support

Customer satisfaction is hard to quantify, but OKRs attempt to do that.

Example:

Objective: Improve the support team's performance

Key results:

- Conducting two training sessions before the end of the Quarter
- Increasing team personal target score to 85%
- Ensuring at least 95% of the department members reach the target before the end of the quarter

Generally, regardless of the department, OKRs should be properly defined because they dictate every process and action performed in a company. OKRs help to improve individual performance and, by extension, contribute to the achievement of ultimate goals by enabling different teams to work together.

Chapter 12. Best OKRs Tools and Software

In large organizations, spreadsheets may prove to be inadequate as OKRs management and maintenance tools. Small companies can use spreadsheets, but with company growth and an increase in complexity of company functions, advanced tools will need to be utilized when implementing the OKRs.

OKRs tools are a critical and significant part of the OKR framework. A good OKRs tool or software will seamlessly align with the workings of a company and reinforce best practices that are already established while adapting to changes and complexities occasioned by improved performance and growth.

Attributes of a Good OKRs Software or Tool

- User Interface (UI): The software should have a clean and attractive UI. A good interface will make the software easy to use by all employees.

- Usability: The tool is easy to use and is accompanied by tutorials, training, and user support to ensure the software can be used by anyone in the organization.

- Goal maps: The tool should tie in the organization's OKRs to the key results. It aligns individual responsibilities with company objectives that employees are tasked with achieving.

- Features and functionality: Enables the staff to evaluate their performance and communicate with each other so that they meet the set goals.

- Reporting and insights: The software should be made to create reports on the progress of the OKRs, the rates of change, and analysis reports of what objectives and teams are facing challenges.

- Integration: The software should work well with all the software and the systems that are already in use in the organization. The software will need to be linked to management systems, HR software, and sales software, among others.

- Customizable: The tool or software should have ready templates that can be used for customization in line with the organizations' needs and requirements.

- Value: Good software has a cost that is proportional to the software capabilities, installation, and maintenance.

Benefits of OKRs Software and Tools

1. They help facilitate the OKR framework. They offer support and make the OKRs easy to implement and maintain.

2. OKR software and tools make it easier to track the progress made when trying to meet set targets.

3. They help with the creation of effective OKRs and keeping them up to date. They help keep the key results updated and actionable.

Considerations When Choosing OKRs Software and Tools

A good OKR software or tool should:

- Be easy to use
- Suit the company, i.e., should match the scale of the company
- Reinforce company practices
- Be flexible. This will allow the tool to accommodate the changes in the organization

- Collect frequent feedback
- Allow sharing of OKRs in the company
- Highlight arising problems with the OKRs

OKRs Software and Tools

The OKRs software and tools can be used for goal management and tracking of teams, individuals, and organizations.

Types of OKRs tools:

- Free- such as spreadsheets. They can be used to manage the OKRs using readily available templates that can be modified to the organization's needs.

- Paid tools- These are tools specifically used to manage OKRs in an organization. They are useful in companies that are already large or small businesses that are seeing growth at a fast rate. An OKR tool makes managing OKRs, individuals, and teams working on them easier.

The following are some examples of OKRs tools available on the market:

1. Profit. Co

It is user-friendly. It has a good interface with a dashboard that shows tracking metrics such as the task progress. Profit.co accommodates employee engagement and development, strategy tracking, and task management. It can accommodate 1-5 year strategic initiatives.

Profit.co is customizable, and modules can be added to accommodate growing company needs. This OKR tool is popular with Microsoft teams and Hub Spot, among many others. The cost of this tool is quite affordable.

Profit.co is preferred because it offers step guides and templates, facilitates departmental review meetings, and includes OKR certification and coaching.

However, profit.co is only available in a few languages (15). Its feature options could prove overwhelming to many and only has 30 integrations.

2. Unlock: OKR

This tool is best used by teams that are implementing OKRs for the first time. The dashboard, in this case, will display team member progress, insights among other OKR progress.

Unlock: OKR is aimed at helping organizations work towards a shared vision and plan. Unlock: OKR provides pricing when requested, a demo, and a free trial.

Pros:

The simple user interface, easy to implement and offers coaching on how it should be used.

Cons:

The existing OKR cannot be cloned, and email is not integrated.

3. PeopleGoal

This OKRs tool is mostly used by HR departments. It has been used by companies such as Shell and Formula 1. The design of this tool is reminiscent of Google-made products.

Pros:

- It supports different office sites such as Ms teams, Ms Azure, AWS, among others

- It has a robust reporting site
- It can be customized
- It has planning tools

Cons:

- A mobile app has not yet been developed
- Some integrations are only made available in the enterprise plan

4. **Simple OKR**

This tool is best suited for work culture research. This tool accommodates team OKRs, personal OKRs, and company OKRs.

Pros:

Easy to use, has a good UI that shows progress reports, aligns the objectives across the users, and organizes objectives into sub-objectives that can be broken down into more manageable tasks.

Cons:

It has fixed pricing and does not accommodate third-party software integrations.

5. **Yaguara**

This is the most preferred OKR software for e-retail. It is a tool that is focused on data-driven projects that are related to the businesses' goals and objectives.

Yaguara excels at unifying and integrating with other software and platforms such as; Facebook, Shopify, Google Ads, among others.

Pros:

User-friendly, has good communication tools and is great when it comes to agile e-commerce teams.

Cons:

Customizable integration is only available for the enterprise plan. Reports and dashboards also have the same limitation.

The OKRs framework requires a good tool to support it to align business strategies and objectives across collaborating individuals and teams, to ensure that objectives end up with desired results.

Manual tracking of OKRs is convenient for small enterprises but very challenging for medium and large organizations. OKRs tools and software simplify the management of performance and the OKRs framework in bigger businesses where the process is more complex.

SECTION 5

CASE STUDIES, SUCCESS STORIES, AND CONCLUSION

Success Stories

My Personal OKRs

April 2020, my weight was 105 kgs. I was failing with weight loss for the last 30 years. I had consulted numerous dieticians and consultants, read 10s of books, but nothing seemed to work.

The magic of OKR is setting 90 days goals, setting key metrics for results (KRs). List down action points to achieve those results in 90 days and keep monitoring every week.

My Objective – Perfect Health by 30th June 2020

Key Results –

- 80 kg Weight
- Fasting Sugar 100, HBA1c – 5.5, and all other parameters within normal range

Action Points

1. Low carb diet (no sugar, rice, wheat, grains, bread, and alcohol). Only proteins, vegetables, and salads

2. 5km walk every day

3. Every Sunday, weight training

Weekly Check-ins

- Every Sunday, I will take my weight and body measurements, Check my sugar levels, and not it down in my tracking sheet.

- I was able to know what is working and what is not working.

By the end of June, I achieved the following Key Results

- My weight was 78kg,

- Fasting sugar 105,

- HBA1c -5.5

- All other parameters normal.

- In fact, my new, very large insurance policy went through without any objections from underwriters. My Insurance adviser told me I was the only one above 60 whose policy went through. Rest all were rejected due to some of the other medical complications.

Success Story with an SME Client

He was one of the biggest brands in fitness equipment. His sales were declining for the last two years.

Outlined below were the OKRs decided after brainstorming with the team for around 15 days in November 2020 for the period November 2020 to February 2021.

We appointed one ambassador who was responsible for driving the OKRs and keep track of all the results.

Since their only challenge was the sales; we worked out OKRs around sales only

Objective – Grow Sales Exponentially

Key Results –

1. Grow the offline and online sales by 100% as compared to the previous quarter

Action Points

1. Discuss OKRs with the entire sales team and come up with total sales goals for the quarter and also sales goals for each individual rep.

2. Close coordination with the digital marketing team to double the sales in 90 days

Weekly Check-ins

- We started meeting every week with the sales team and digital marketing team and discuss the achievements and challenges.

- We started keeping the score for every individual sales executive and the entire team.

- We kept on discussing strategies for what is working and what is not working.

Results

- We were able to achieve around 85% growth in sales in 90 days.

- At the end of the quarter, we celebrated with the teams. We organized lunch and awarded the sales teams.

- In the end, the whole team was fully charged up and motivated. They were following each and every lead on a regular basis. Also proactively asking referrals from existing clients. Also calling old clients and they started getting repeat orders from the,

- We set more ambitious goals for the next quarter.

Case Studies

Case Study 1: MY Exporter Client

Their challenge was stagnant sales and profits for the last three years.

After brainstorming with the founders and key employees, we started working on sales only. We appointed an OKR champion who would drive OKRs and keep track of progress.

Objective –

Grow sales and profits

Key Results –

- Double the sales in first 90 days as compared to the previous year
- Grow Gross Profit and Net profit by 75% in 90 Days

Action Points

- Follow up on every lead diligently
- Attend four new international fairs
- Send offer to all the old database of clients

Weekly Check-ins

Results
- Sale growth by 70%
- Net profit growth seven times

This year we again saw the dip in sales due to Pandemic, but we were able to maintain decent sales and net profit.

The team is highly motivated and fully charged up to keep on achieving new highs post-pandemic.

Case Study 2: My Group Coaching Participants

I started the OKR experiment with a group of 30+ participants who are professionals and small business owners and set their OKRs starting November 2020 to February 2021.

Objectives – Double your Revenue

Key Results – 100% revenue growth in 90 days for everyone compared to the previous year

Action Points –

- Everyone decided their own action points and all OKRs and Action points were recorded on a centralized google spreadsheet
- Everybody selected their accountability partners from the group, and they were checking with each other on their OKRs and action points

Results

At the end of the quarter in February 2021, over 70% of participants were able to double their revenue in 90days. Many of them improved their health.

Few couldn't achieve this because they were inconsistent in their weekly check-ins and follow-up with an accountability partner.

Now, there is no looking back. Companies and individuals have lined up to implement OKRs for their business and personal goals. Demand on my time is much more than I can handle.

Hence, I decided to write this book and spread the knowledge about OKRs to every SME business owner in the world.

Don't read this book like a novel. Read each chapter at least two times and make notes. Implement each and every learning from this book in real life.

Post your reviews on Amazon and show your love. Thank you. All the best for your amazing future

You can reach me at:

suresh@sureshmansharamani.com
www.sureshmansharamani.com
https://www.linkedin.com/in/smramani/
https://www.facebook.com/SMansharamani
Instagram @suresh_mansharamani_coach
https://www.youtube.com/channel/UCjd7Hr17wfg5-xwcMYhyEpQ

Other Books by Suresh Mansharamani

1. https://www.amazon.com/Lose-Reverse-Your-Diabetes-Days ebook/dp/B08K3MBJJN/ref=sr_1_4?dchild=1&keywords=sure sh+mansharamani&qid=1620976237&s=books&sr=1-4
2. https://www.amazon.com/Closing-Your-Sales-Ultimate-Guide- ebook/dp/B083WLKDCG/ref=sr_1_3?dchild=1&keywords=sur esh+mansharamani&qid=1620976237&s=books&sr=1-3
3. https://www.amazon.com/Super-Power-Networker-Blueprint-Networking- ebook/dp/B08Z7P5BXS/ref=sr_1_2?dchild=1&keywords=sures h+mansharamani&qid=1620976237&s=books&sr=1-2
4. https://www.amazon.com/Own-Stage-Master-Public-Speaking- ebook/dp/B07YXB4M5G/ref=sr_1_1?dchild=1&keywords=sure sh+mansharamani&qid=1620976237&s=books&sr=1-1

Conclusion

If you want a structured and proven goals setting method to unlock your potential and help you boost your performance and results, objectives and key results methodology is the way to go.

As you have learned in the book, the OKRs framework is a simple but effective performance and outcome management tool which guides everyone in an organization to track progress and align their tasks toward achieving common goals.

Individuals and organizations are always striving to outperform themselves and the only way to consistently achieve growth is to inspire better performance. OKRs is great at pushing people out of their comfort zones to achieve more than they are used to by defining and setting specific and measurable actions for specific outcomes, and monitoring and reporting progress for everyone to see.

More importantly, OKRs can are powerful for planning long-term goals by setting objectives to lead you to what you want to achieve, and then break it down into key results to get you to the results you envision. It is the ultimate goal-setting methodology because it introduces culture and mental shift in the way we approach goal setting and the way we execute strategy, from concentrating on work to emphasizing outcomes.

OKRs has proven that better results are guaranteed through open collaboration within an organization. Rather than the traditional top-down approach where goals are dictated from the top, OKRs is all involving and is an amalgam of top-down and bottom-up approaches to strategic planning and execution. An organization is better off with everyone contributing to and buying into the vision- OKRs ensure that individuals and teams pull in the same direction which is not very easy to do.

OKRs guarantee organizations four main benefits in the implementation and execution of strategy:

- The alignment of individuals and teams to the ultimate goal alleviates the complexities of departmental isolation.

- Better performance accountability since OKRs allow for objective tracking of individual goals which translates to easier decision making for roles and responsibilities.

- Improved corporate direction because it allows for quick identification of inadequacies and modifications to correct strategic course.

- Highly motivated employees since everyone has a clearly defined goal to work towards which is aligned to the main goals.

OKRs strategy means greater focus and alignment of goals to strategy, and improved transparency by coalescing teams and their respective responsibilities to accomplish common objectives.

Objectives and key results work for individuals and teams and similarly transforms small and big businesses. OKRs have no room for complacency as much as they are accommodative and adaptable-this is the goal setting system for anyone or company yearning for inspiration and guidance to perform better than they have been doing.

Resources

I have created a playlist and recorded around 16 videos on OKRs which will be very useful for you.

Here is the link to my playlist on YouTube
https://youtube.com/playlist?list=PLT5WzgO6pPynNJR23hTAfTap4UxzolOjo

www.ingramcontent.com/pod-product-compliance
Lightning Source LLC
Chambersburg PA
CBHW051428150726
48000CB00005B/2003